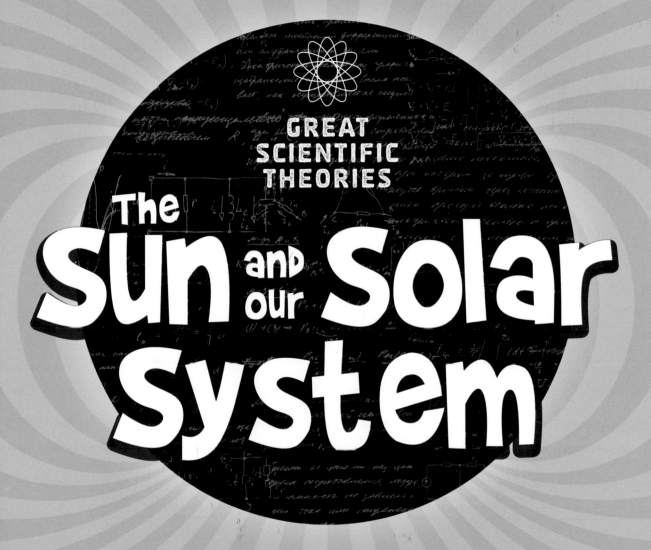

GREAT SCIENTIFIC THEORIES

The Sun and our Solar System

Jen Green

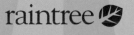
raintree

a Capstone company — publishers for children

Raintree is an imprint of Capstone Global Library Limited, a company incorporated in England and Wales having its registered office at 264 Banbury Road, Oxford, OX2 7DY – Registered company number: 6695582

www.raintree.co.uk
myorders@raintree.co.uk

Edited by Helen Cox Cannons
Designed by Terri Poburka
Original illustrations © Capstone Global Library Limited 2017
Picture research by Morgan Walters
Production by Steve Walker
Originated by Capstone Global Library Limited
Printed and bound in China

ISBN 978 1 4747 4607 6
21 20 19 18 17
10 9 8 7 6 5 4 3 2 1

British Library Cataloguing in Publication Data
A full catalogue record for this book is available from the British Library.

Acknowledgements
We would like to thank the following for permission to reproduce photographs: Alamy Stock Photo: PjrTravel, 24; Dreamstime: Nicku, 17; Capstone Press: Terri Poburka, 6; Getty Images: Hulton Archive, 18, Leemage, 23, Stock Montage, 7; iStockphoto: ZU_09, 25; Library of Congress, 8; Newscom: akg-images, 16, akg-images, 19, akg-images/Stefan Arczynski, 13, Album, 10, Oxford Science Archive Heritage Images, 14, Pictures From History, 21, 22, World History Archive, 9; Shutterstock: Alexander_P, (telescope) 28, Arevik, (paper) design element throughout, creativemarc, 27, Dimedrol68, 11, fixer00, (stripes) design element, Golden Shrimp, design element, hideto999, Cover, MarcelClemens, 26, Nikolayenko Yekaterina, (moon) 28, pablofdezr, 5, Senoldo, (stars) 28, Stavrida, 15, Triff, 4, Victor Josan, 20; Wikimedia: Raven, 12.

We would like to thank Dr Rohini Giles at NASA's Jet Propulsion Laboratory for her invaluable help in the preparation of this book.

Every effort has been made to contact copyright holders of material reproduced in this book. Any omissions will be rectified in subsequent printings if notice is given to the publisher.

All the internet addresses (URLs) given in this book were valid at the time of going to press. However, due to the dynamic nature of the internet, some addresses may have changed, or sites may have changed or ceased to exist since publication. While the author and publisher regret any inconvenience this may cause readers, no responsibility for any such changes can be accepted by either the author or the publisher.

CONTENTS

Some words are shown in bold, **like this**.
You can find out what they mean by
looking in the glossary.

IDEAS ABOUT THE SOLAR SYSTEM

Science is about finding out how things work. That includes not just the world around us, but the Universe, which is everything that exists. We now know the Universe is so vast it's hard to imagine. But long ago, people thought our tiny corner of the Universe was the whole of space.

Scientific ideas

For hundreds of years, scientists have tried to explain things by coming up with ideas about the way things work. These scientific ideas are known as hypotheses. When scientists believe they have collected enough **evidence** to show that their idea is correct, the idea becomes a **theory**.

The Sun is the centre of our solar system.

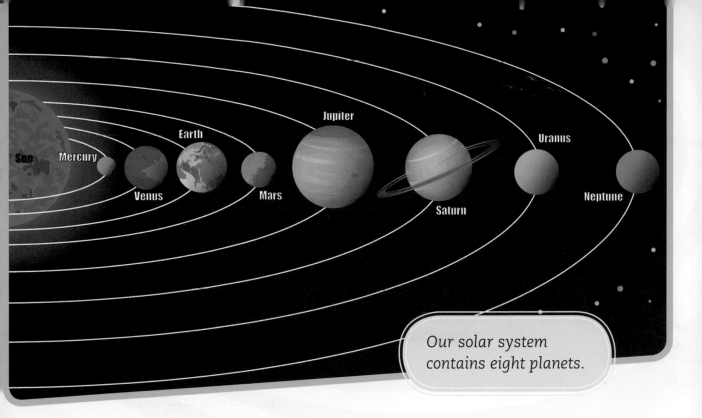

Sun   Mercury   Earth   Jupiter   Uranus

Venus   Mars   Saturn   Neptune

Our solar system contains eight planets.

What is the solar system?

Our **solar system** is the Sun and everything that moves around it. That includes planets, their **moons** and billions of chunks of rock and ice. These circle the Sun in paths called **orbits**.

Sun at the centre

We now know the Sun is the centre of our solar system. But for hundreds of years, people thought Earth was at the centre. After all, from the planet's surface, Earth seems to be still, and the Sun, Moon and stars wheel across the sky. Then a few scientists dared to disagree. This book looks at these scientists and their theories.

Sun and planets

Our solar system includes eight planets. Those nearest to the Sun are Mercury, Venus, Earth and Mars. These relatively small planets are all made of rock and metal. There are four giant outer planets: Jupiter, Saturn, Uranus and Neptune. These are mostly made of gas and liquid.

EARTH-CENTRED UNIVERSE

Astronomy is the study of the stars and other objects in the heavens. From the earliest times, people were in wonder of the night sky.

The first astronomers

Four thousand years ago, the Babylonians (people who lived in what is now Iraq) studied the night sky. They named the groups of stars that wheeled above them. We now call these star groups **constellations**. In ancient times, travellers used constellations to find their way.

The Babylonians thought the heavens arched over a flat Earth.

Planets

Babylonian astronomers noticed five "stars" which acted strangely. They wandered across the sky instead of moving in fixed patterns. We now know these are **planets**. They don't truly shine like stars, but reflect sunlight. The five planets known in ancient times were Mercury, Venus, Mars, Jupiter and Saturn.

Greek thinkers

About 2,500 years ago, the ancient Greeks began to think about the world more scientifically. A thinker called Pythagoras suggested the world was not flat, but ball-shaped. He had noticed that ships heading out to sea disappeared over the horizon. The Greeks still believed Earth was the centre of the Universe. The philosopher Aristotle (384–322 BC) wrote that Earth was fixed, and the Sun, Moon and stars circled around it.

ARISTOTLE'S PUPIL

Aristotle was the tutor of a young Greek prince named Alexander. The boy grew up to become a great warrior. Alexander the Great conquered a vast empire, stretching from Greece to India and south into Egypt. In the conquered lands, he founded cities, which were all named Alexandria after him.

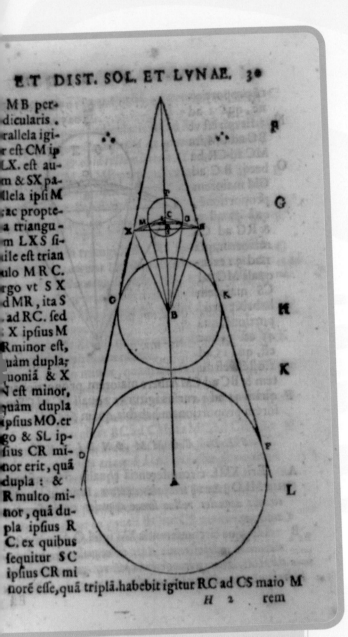

Aristarchus tried to work out the sizes of the Moon (top), Earth and Sun (bottom).

A lone voice

Aristotle's Earth-centred view of the Universe was accepted by nearly everyone. But one man thought differently. He was called Aristarchus (about 310–230 BC) and he came from the small Greek island of Samos.

Sun at the centre

Aristarchus thought that the Sun, not Earth, was the centre of the Universe. Earth moved around the Sun, not the other way around. He also thought that the stars were very far away. This meant that the Universe was much bigger than people had thought.

Alexandria

Aristarchus moved from Samos to Alexandria in Egypt, which was part of the Greek world. Alexandria had become a great centre for learning, and had the world's finest library. In Alexandria, Aristarchus talked with other **scholars**, but almost no one accepted his idea.

Ptolemy of Alexandria

In the 2nd century BC, the Romans took over the Greek world. They also took over Greek learning. In Alexandria, a scholar named Ptolemy (AD 85–165) collected all the Greek ideas about astronomy and put them into one big book called the *Great Treatise*. Ptolemy's book repeated Aristotle's view of an Earth-centred universe. Aristarchus's idea was forgotten.

This illustration shows Ptolemy observing the stars. He is using an instrument called a quadrant.

PTOLEMY'S BOOK

In the 4th century AD, the Roman Empire was attacked by northern tribes. The great library of Alexandria burned to the ground during a battle. Luckily, Ptolemy's book had been copied, or it would have been lost forever. One copy was translated into Arabic. Arab scholars called it the *Almagest*, which simply means "the Greatest".

A REVOLUTIONARY IDEA

In the 1100s, Ptolemy's book was translated into European languages. It soon became the main textbook for **astronomy**. **Scholars** everywhere accepted Aristotle's view that Earth was the centre of the Universe. Everyone, that is, until a Polish astronomer called Nicolaus Copernicus (1473–1543) challenged the idea.

NICOLAUS COPERNICUS

Copernicus was very well-educated. He had spent 12 years at university in Poland and then Italy, studying law, medicine, mathematics and astronomy. In Italy, he lodged with the professor of astronomy Domenico Navara. Every night the two studied the stars and Copernicus became a keen astronomer.

A passion for astronomy

Copernicus lived in a town in northern Poland. A clever and able man, he worked as a **canon** in the **Roman Catholic Church**. This involved many different jobs. By day, Copernicus worked as a lawyer, doctor and administrator. But his real passion was astronomy. Every night, he studied the stars from a little tower that was his **observatory**.

Observing the heavens

At this time, there were no telescopes or binoculars. So Copernicus relied on just his eyes. He used mathematical tables to work out the positions of the stars and **planets**. These tables were based on Ptolemy's work. He also had various instruments. One was an **armillary sphere**. This was a moveable model of the heavens, with interlocking rings surrounding a ball at the centre. The rings represented the **orbits** of the Moon, Sun and planets, and the ball represented Earth.

This is an armillary sphere. Astronomers adjusted the rings to measure the positions of the planets and stars relative to the Earth.

Crystal spheres

For many years, Copernicus observed the night sky from his little tower. As he did, he became more and more frustrated with the traditional view of the Universe. According to Aristotle, Earth was surrounded by a series of **transparent spheres** made of crystal. The inner sphere with the Moon was surrounded by spheres carrying the Sun and planets. The outer sphere with the stars marked the edge of the Universe. But what Copernicus saw just didn't fit the model or the accepted view of space.

This illustration shows a man crawling under the edge of the sky to look at the heavens. People simply did not know what was beyond the sky.

Problems

One problem was that the planets seemed to move to and fro, and sometimes went backwards, instead of circling neatly. Astronomers had tried to explain this by saying the planets moved in smaller circles inside their spheres. They also said Earth was not exactly at the centre. It had all become incredibly complicated. There had to be another explanation.

Breakthrough moment

NEW THINKING

In a flash, Copernicus realized that the Sun, not Earth, was at the centre of the solar system, and Earth and that the planets circled around it. This **theory** is known as heliocentrism. Aristarchus had been right all those years ago. If Earth circled the Sun, it had to be a planet. And if the Sun and stars did not move across the sky, Earth itself had to be turning at high speed. So why couldn't people feel it turning? Copernicus reckoned that if the **atmosphere** was also turning, you wouldn't notice the **rotation**. This idea turned out to be right.

Copernicus realizes the true structure of the solar system.

Going against the Church

Copernicus realized that his heliocentrism idea would cause a revolution in astronomy. But there was an even bigger problem. His idea went against the teaching of the powerful Roman Catholic Church. This was particularly awkward for Copernicus as a man of the Church.

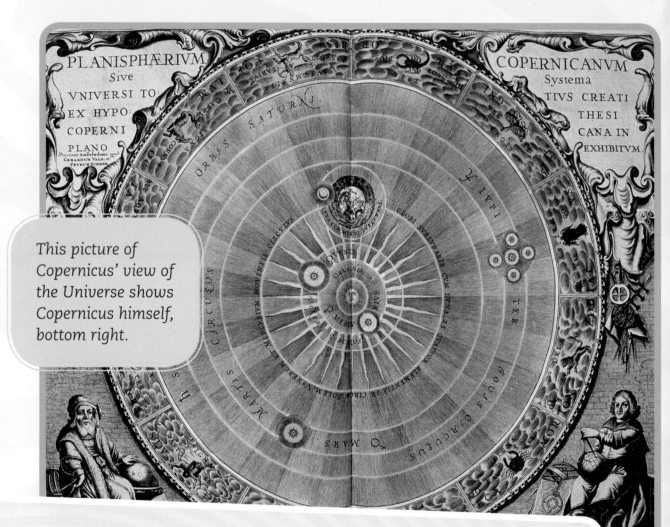

This picture of Copernicus' view of the Universe shows Copernicus himself, bottom right.

CHRISTIAN VIEW OF THE UNIVERSE

Christian teaching on the Universe was based on the Bible. The Old Testament said that God had "fixed the earth, firm and immovable". This fitted with Aristotle's theory. If you disagreed with Church teaching, you could be accused of a crime called **heresy**. If found guilty, you could be tied to a wooden stake and burned to death.

In secret

Copernicus became very frightened about what would happen if his idea became widely known. So he kept it quiet. For 30 years, he carried on with his work as a doctor and lawyer. Secretly, he continued making **observations**. All this **evidence** went into a great book, which he called *On the Revolutions of the Heavenly Spheres*. But he did not publish this book.

In print

In 1538, a young German professor named Georg Rheticus read a small booklet by Copernicus. He realized it was a breakthrough. He travelled to Poland and became Copernicus' assistant. He persuaded Copernicus, who was now old and sick, to let him arrange for the book to be published. The story goes that he placed the book in the old man's hands as he lay dying.

This statue shows Copernicus holding an armillary sphere.

HOW PLANETS MOVE

Copernicus' book was a major leap forward in our understanding of the Universe. Luckily, it was not immediately banned as he had feared it would be. News of his **theory** spread among astronomers. It soon reached a leading Danish astronomer called Tycho Brahe (1546–1601).

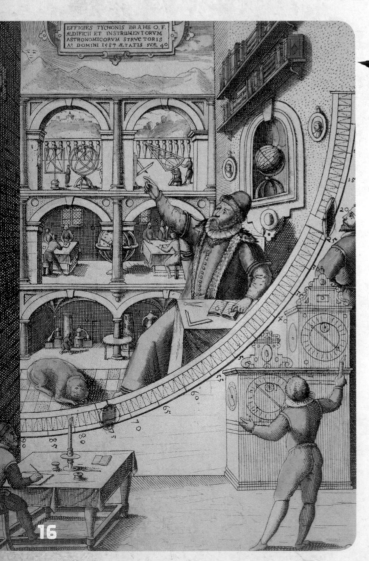

TYCHO BRAHE

Tycho Brahe was a Danish nobleman. As a young man, his nose had been badly damaged in a **duel**. Afterwards he had to wear a metal nose. He was known as the "man with the golden nose". In the 1570s, the Danish king had built him an **observatory** on a tiny island between Denmark and Sweden. It was equipped with all the latest instruments. Brahe spent over 20 years there observing the night sky.

Tycho's test

Brahe asked his assistant, Johannes Kepler (1571–1630), to test the new theory against the old model. Kepler was a brilliant young German professor of mathematics. Brahe asked him to **predict** the positions of the planets using tables based on Ptolemy and Copernicus.

A new shape for orbits

Kepler found that Copernicus' system worked quite well, but was still not completely accurate. He realized this was because Copernicus had thought that the planets moved in perfect circles. Kepler realized that their **orbits** were slightly oval. This shape is called an **ellipse**. Kepler published his findings on the planets' movements. Sure enough, when he included the ellipse in his calculations, his predictions were correct.

Johannes Kepler

GALILEO'S TELESCOPE

By 1600, Copernicus's **theory** was still not widely accepted. What was needed was some sort of proof that people could see with their own eyes. The great Italian scientist Galileo Galilei (1564–1642) would provide this proof.

A young professor

Galileo was professor of mathematics at the Italian university of Padua. As well as maths, he also loved natural sciences (what we would now call physics) and was always experimenting.

Experiments

Most **scholars** of the day believed everything Aristotle said was right, but not Galileo. Aristotle had said that heavy objects fall faster than light ones. Galileo is said to have tested this by dropping two metal balls of different weights from the Leaning Tower of Pisa! The balls hit the ground at the same time. This story may not be true. But his work showed that even the great Aristotle could be wrong.

Galileo tests Aristotle's theory about the speed of falling objects.

A new invention

In 1609, Galileo heard that a Dutch spectacle-maker had invented an instrument to **magnify** distant objects (make them look larger). The instrument, called a telescope, was a long tube containing two lenses. Someone described it to Galileo. He quickly worked out how to make one for himself. Then he turned it on the heavens. What he saw there would change ideas about the **solar system** forever.

THE FIRST TELESCOPES

Dutch spectacle-maker Hans Lippershey is said to have invented the telescope after children playing in his workshop discovered you could see distant objects if you put two lenses together. Galileo's telescope was 10 times more powerful than Lippershey's. It made things about 30 times larger than they were in real life.

Galileo's telescopes

Through Galileo's telescope

Galileo's telescope amazed everyone who used it, and he was soon making more for wealthy people. Rich merchants used them to look at ships far out to sea. Galileo was more excited by what he saw in the sky at night.

Jupiter's moons

Galileo's telescope showed that the planets were bright discs, not points of light. He saw four tiny lights moving around the planet **Jupiter**. Night after night, they changed position. He realized they were **moons** – the first ever discovered beyond Earth's Moon.

Callisto

Europa

Ganymede

Io

JUPITER

Galileo discovered Jupiter's largest four moons: Io, Europa, Ganymede and Callisto.

Looking at Venus

Galileo got another surprise when he turned his telescope on the planet Venus. Over several weeks, he saw different amounts of the planet's surface were lit by the Sun. We now know that the same thing happens to the Moon as it **orbits** Earth – the sunlit part grows and shrinks. It could only mean that Venus was orbiting the Sun. Copernicus was right.

Galileo demonstrates his telescope to noblemen in Venice.

Starry Messenger

Galileo published his discoveries in a book called *Starry Messenger*. The book was a great success, and he got many new orders for telescopes. However, the **Roman Catholic Church** was not pleased that Galileo said Copernicus was right.

Breakthrough moment

GALILEO'S DISCOVERIES

Galileo made discoveries about the Moon's surface. Scholars had said it was smooth, but Galileo saw mountains and huge craters. When he focused his telescope on the stars, they still looked like points of light. This meant they were very far away. What's more, there were hundreds of new stars, which no one had ever seen before with just their eyes.

A warning

In 1616, the Catholic Church banned Copernicus' book. The **Pope** said that Earth was the fixed centre of the Universe. Just 16 years before, a scholar called Giordano Bruno had been burned at the stake for **heresy**. He had claimed that Earth moved around the Sun and the stars were distant suns. The Church was against these new scientific theories.

A new Pope

In 1623, the Pope died and a new Pope, Urban VIII, was chosen. Urban VIII allowed Galileo to write a book about the issue. But he said Galileo had to express both sides of the argument: that the Sun and planets orbited Earth, and alternatively that the Sun lay at the centre. When the book was published, it was clear Galileo agreed with Copernicus. This made the Pope angry, and Galileo was arrested for heresy.

Galileo as an old man

This painting shows Galileo (centre) facing trial for defending the theories of Copernicus.

Galileo's trial

In 1632, the Church put Galileo on trial. He was now an old man of 68. He was forced to kneel and swear on the Bible that Earth, not the Sun, lay at the centre, and Earth did not move. As he got up, he is said to have muttered, "And yet it does move".

Prison sentence

Galileo was found guilty of heresy. He was **sentenced** to prison. But in the end, he was allowed to live in his own home as long as he kept quiet. He continued with his experiments for the rest of his life. Despite the Church's view, people gradually accepted that Copernicus was right.

UNDERSTANDING THE SOLAR SYSTEM

Galileo showed that the **planets orbit** the Sun. But why? The answer is **gravity**. This force was discovered by the English scientist Sir Isaac Newton (1643–1727).

Newton also invented a powerful new telescope that used mirrors instead of lenses to focus light.

What is gravity?

Gravity is the force that pulls objects towards one another. The heavier the object, the bigger the pull. The Sun is the heaviest object in the **solar system**, so Newton knew it had to be at the centre.

Scale of the Universe

In Newton's time, many people still thought the Universe did not stretch far beyond the solar system. In the 1700s, scientists realized the Universe was far, far bigger than people had imagined. This was partly due to the German-born astronomer called William Herschel (1738–1822).

William Herschel

Herschel was a keen amateur astronomer who made telescopes. In 1781, he discovered a new planet, which was named Uranus. He also discovered thousands of new stars and star clusters.

HUGE TELESCOPES!

Herschel started out by renting a telescope. However, he decided he wanted a bigger telescope, so he began to make his own. His telescopes got larger and larger – the biggest one was 12 metres (40 feet) long!

The Milky Way

By counting stars in different parts of the sky, Herschel realized that our solar system was part of the huge **galaxy** we call the Milky Way. This looks like a dense trail of stars across the sky. Herschel thought that our solar system lay at the centre of this disc-shaped galaxy. In fact, it is located on one of the arms that spiral outwards.

New discoveries

Astronomers are always finding out more about space. In 1846, the planet Neptune was discovered beyond Uranus. This brought the number of planets in the solar system to eight.

The stars

In the 1900s, astronomers studied the stars using ever more powerful telescopes. They developed methods of rating stars by their size and brightness. This helped us to realize the enormous distances between stars.

Expanding Universe

In the 1920s, American astronomer Edwin Hubble (1889–1953) studied distant galaxies. Hubble realized that galaxies are moving apart at great speed. This shows that the Universe is getting bigger. Scientists now believe the Universe began in a great explosion of energy. We call this the Big Bang.

The Hubble Space Telescope is named after the American astronomer. It allows us to study distant galaxies.

HUBBLE'S GALAXIES

Edwin Hubble worked at the Mount Wilson **Observatory** in western United States. This contained what was then the world's most powerful telescope. Hubble realized that there were several main shapes of galaxies. Many, like the Milky Way, are shaped like spirals. Others are ball-shaped, or irregular.

Life elsewhere?

Scientists now know that the Universe stretches far, far beyond our solar system. Astronomers believe that the Universe contains at least 100 billion galaxies. Each of these contains billions of stars. No life has been discovered yet beyond planet Earth. But the Universe is so vast that scientists believe it must exist somewhere, on other planets circling other stars.

This view of the galaxy M101 was taken by the Hubble Space Telescope. It is thought to contain around 1 trillion stars.

QUIZ

1. Which ancient people kept the first written records of the stars and **planets**?

2. How many planets were known to ancient people (not counting Earth)?

3. Which ancient Greek thinker suggested that Earth was shaped like a ball?

4. What did Aristotle believe lay at the centre of the Universe?

5. Who was the first thinker to suggest Earth moved around the Sun?

6. Which writer based in Egypt collected Greek knowledge of **astronomy** into a big book?

7. Which German professor persuaded Copernicus to publish his book?

8. Which astronomer had an **observatory** built specially for him on a small island?

9. Do planets move around the Sun in perfect circles?

10. Who made the first telescope?

11. Which Italian astronomer discovered mountains and craters on the Moon?

12. Which English scientist discovered **gravity**?

13. What planet was discovered by William Herschel?

14. Who discovered the Universe is expanding?

For the answers to this quiz, see page 31

TIMELINE

about 2300 BC The ancient Babylonians keep the first records of the stars.

about 550 BC The Greek thinker Pythagoras suggests the Earth is shaped like a ball.

about 330 BC The Greek philosopher Aristotle states that Earth is the centre of the Universe.

3rd century BC Aristarchus of Samos suggests that Earth moves around the Sun.

about AD 150 Ptolemy of Alexandria includes all Greek knowledge of **astronomy** in a book.

1543 Polish astronomer Nicolaus Copernicus publishes *On the Revolutions of the Heavenly Spheres*. This suggests that the Earth moves around the Sun.

1608 Dutch spectacle-maker Hans Lippershey invents the telescope.

1609 Johannes Kepler describes the movements of the planets.

1610 Galileo publishes *Starry Messenger*, which describes what he observed through his telescope.

1616 The **Roman Catholic Church** bans Copernicus' book.

1632 Galileo is found guilty of **heresy** for saying that Earth moves around the Sun.

1687 Sir Isaac Newton publishes his laws of **gravity**.

1781 William Herschel discovers the planet Uranus using his 12-metre- (40 foot-) long telescope.

1929 Edwin Hubble discovers the Universe is expanding.

1990 The Hubble Space Telescope starts to take pictures of distant galaxies.

GLOSSARY

armillary sphere moveable model of the heavens

astronomy study of the stars, planets, moons and other objects in space. People who study stars and planets are called astronomers.

atmosphere layer of gases surrounding a planet such as Earth

canon official of the Church

constellation arrangement of stars, as seen from Earth

duel fight with weapons such as pistols or swords

ellipse oval-shaped path

evidence collection of information or facts that prove if something is true or not

galaxy enormous group of stars

gravity force that pulls objects towards each other. Gravity keeps the planets orbiting the Sun, and the Moon orbiting Earth

heresy idea that goes against the teachings of the Church

magnify make something seem bigger

moon large object in space that orbits a planet

observation closely monitoring or studying something

observatory building where astronomers use telescopes to study the stars

orbit path of a planet or star around a larger body, such as the Sun

Pope leader of the Roman Catholic Church

predict expect a certain result

Roman Catholic church Christian church that has the Pope as its head

rotation when an object such as a planet spins around on its axis. An axis is an imaginary line through a planet's northernmost and southernmost point

scholar educated man or woman

sentence punishment set by a court of law

solar system the Sun and all the planets, moons and other debris that circle around it

sphere round, ball-shaped object

theory scientific idea with evidence to back it up

transparent see-through

FIND OUT MORE

BOOKS

Astronomy, Emily Bone (Usborne, 2014)

Solar System (DK Findout!) (Dorling Kindersley, 2016)

Stars and Constellations (The Night Sky: And Other Amazing Sights in Space), Nick Hunter (Heinemann, 2013)

Stars and Planets (Eyewonder) (Dorling Kindersley, 2016)

The Sun (Astronaut Travel Guides), Nick Hunter (Raintree, 2012)

WEBSITES

www.dkfindout.com/uk/science/famous-scientists
There are lots of famous scientists to investigate on this site.
Find out more about Copernicus and Galileo.

www.dkfindout.com/uk/space/solar-system
Find out more about the solar system on this website.

www.esa.int/esaKIDSen/SEMF8WVLWFE_OurUniverse_0.html
This European Space Agency website has fun experiments and the latest news about space exploration.

www.nasa.gov/kidsclub/index.html
The US space agency website includes an interactive site where you can play games and learn about space.

ANSWERS TO QUIZ

1. The Babylonians; **2.** Five: Mercury, Venus, Mars, Jupiter and Saturn; **3.** Pythagoras; **4.** The Earth; **5.** Aristarchus of Samos, in the 3rd century BC; **6.** Ptolemy of Alexandria; **7.** Georg Rheticus; **8.** Tycho Brahe; **9.** No: planets move in stretched-out circles. This shape is called an ellipse; **10.** Dutch spectacle-maker Hans Lippershey; **11.** Galileo; **12.** Sir Isaac Newton; **13.** Uranus; **14.** Edwin Hubble

INDEX